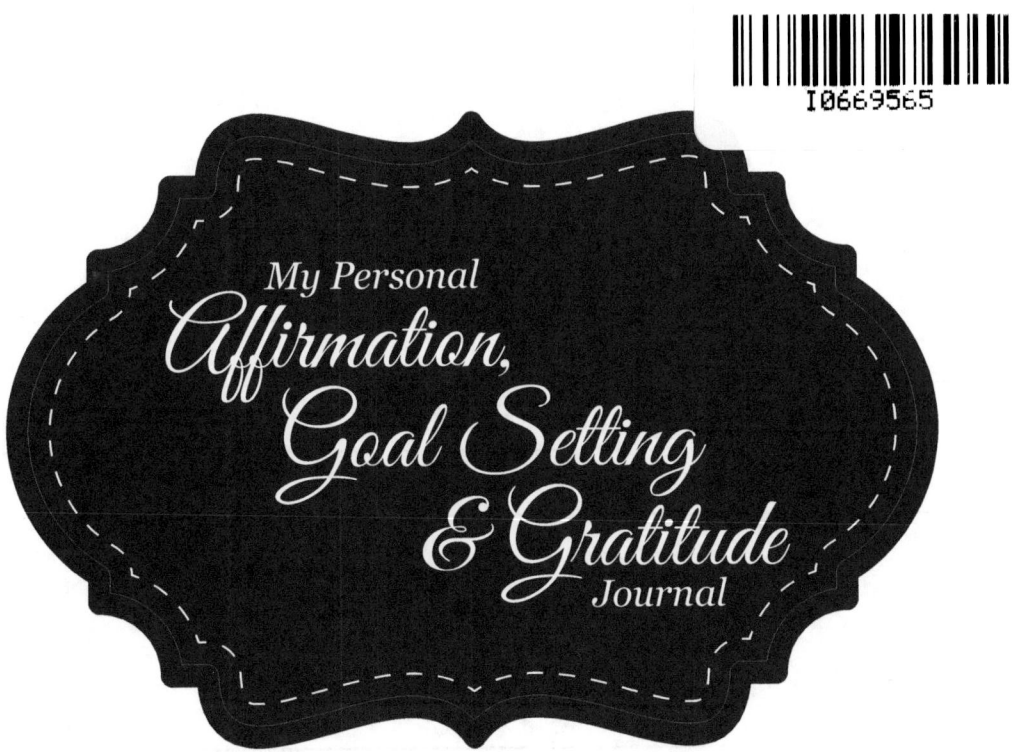

My Personal
Affirmation, Goal Setting & Gratitude
Journal

Gratitude Journal Blank

ACTIVINOTES

Activinotes

DAILY JOURNALS, PLANNERS, NOTEBOOKS AND OTHER BLANK BOOKS

Date: _____

INSIGHTS FOR THE DAY:

_____

_____

_____

_____

_____

NOTES:

_____

_____

_____

_____

_____

_____

_____

_____

_____

_____

_____

_____

_____

_____

_____

_____

My Daily Schedule

today, i must contact...

today, i must do...

notes

6AM

7AM

8AM

9AM

10AM

11AM

12PM

1PM

2PM

3PM

4PM

5PM

6PM

7PM

8PM

My Prayer Journal   date :_____

Confession

_____

Things I'm Thankful for

_____

Prayers for Others

Prayers for Myself

Date: _____

INSIGHTS FOR THE DAY:

_____

_____

_____

_____

_____

NOTES:

_____

_____

_____

_____

_____

_____

_____

_____

_____

_____

_____

_____

_____

_____

_____

My Daily Schedule

today, i must contact...

-
-
-
-
-
-

today, i must do...

-
-
-
-
-
-

notes

6AM

7AM

8AM

9AM

10AM

11AM

12PM

1PM

2PM

3PM

4PM

5PM

6PM

7PM

8PM

My Prayer Journal date :_____

Confession

_____
_____
_____
_____
_____
_____
_____
_____
_____

Things I'm Thankful for

_____
_____
_____
_____
_____
_____
_____
_____
_____
_____

Prayers for Others

_____
_____
_____
_____
_____
_____
_____
_____

Prayers for Myself

_____
_____
_____
_____
_____
_____
_____
_____

Date: _____

INSIGHTS FOR THE DAY:

_____

_____

_____

_____

_____

NOTES:

_____

_____

_____

_____

_____

_____

_____

_____

_____

_____

_____

_____

_____

_____

_____

_____

_____

My Daily Schedule

today, i must contact...

-
-
-
-
-
-

today, i must do...

-
-
-
-
-

notes

6AM

7AM

8AM

9AM

10AM

11AM

12PM

1PM

2PM

3PM

4PM

5PM

6PM

7PM

8PM

My Prayer Journal date :_____

Confession

_____
_____
_____
_____
_____
_____
_____
_____
_____

Things I'm Thankful for

_____
_____
_____
_____
_____
_____
_____
_____
_____

Prayers for Others

_____
_____
_____
_____
_____
_____
_____
_____
_____

Prayers for Myself

_____
_____
_____
_____
_____
_____
_____
_____

Date: _____

INSIGHTS FOR THE DAY:

_____

_____

_____

_____

_____

NOTES:

_____

_____

_____

_____

_____

_____

_____

_____

_____

_____

_____

_____

_____

_____

_____

My Daily Schedule

today, i must contact...

-
-
-
-
-
-

today, i must do...

-
-
-
-
-
-

notes

6AM

7AM

8AM

9AM

10AM

11AM

12PM

1PM

2PM

3PM

4PM

5PM

6PM

7PM

8PM

My Prayer Journal date :_____

Confession

_____
_____
_____
_____
_____
_____
_____
_____
_____

Things I'm Thankful for

_____
_____
_____
_____
_____
_____
_____
_____
_____

Prayers for Others

_____
_____
_____
_____
_____
_____
_____
_____

Prayers for Myself

_____
_____
_____
_____
_____
_____
_____
_____

Date: _____

INSIGHTS FOR THE DAY:

_____

_____

_____

_____

_____

NOTES:

_____

_____

_____

_____

_____

_____

_____

_____

_____

_____

_____

_____

_____

_____

My Daily Schedule

today, i must contact...

-
-
-
-
-
-

today, i must do...

-
-
-
-
-

notes

6AM

7AM

8AM

9AM

10AM

11AM

12PM

1PM

2PM

3PM

4PM

5PM

6PM

7PM

8PM

My Prayer Journal   date :_____

Confession

_____
_____
_____
_____
_____
_____
_____
_____
_____
_____

Things I'm Thankful for

_____
_____
_____
_____
_____
_____
_____
_____
_____
_____

Prayers for Others

_____
_____
_____
_____
_____
_____
_____
_____

Prayers for Myself

_____
_____
_____
_____
_____
_____
_____
_____

INSIGHTS FOR THE DAY:

_____

_____

_____

_____

_____

NOTES:

_____

_____

_____

_____

_____

_____

_____

_____

_____

_____

_____

_____

_____

_____

_____

_____

_____

My Daily Schedule

today, i must contact...

-
-
-
-
-
-

today, i must do...

-
-
-
-
-
-

notes

6AM

7AM

8AM

9AM

10AM

11AM

12PM

1PM

2PM

3PM

4PM

5PM

6PM

7PM

8PM

My Prayer Journal date :_____

Confession

Things I'm Thankful for

Prayers for Others

Prayers for Myself

Date: _____

INSIGHTS FOR THE DAY:

_____

_____

_____

_____

_____

NOTES:

_____

_____

_____

_____

_____

_____

_____

_____

_____

_____

_____

_____

_____

_____

_____

My Daily Schedule

today, i must contact...

-
-
-
-
-

today, i must do...

-
-
-
-
-

notes

6AM

7AM

8AM

9AM

10AM

11AM

12PM

1PM

2PM

3PM

4PM

5PM

6PM

7PM

8PM

My Prayer Journal date :_____

Confession

Things I'm Thankful for

Prayers for Others

Prayers for Myself

Date: _____

INSIGHTS FOR THE DAY:

_____

_____

_____

_____

_____

NOTES:

_____

_____

_____

_____

_____

_____

_____

_____

_____

_____

_____

_____

_____

_____

_____

My Daily Schedule

today, i must contact...

_____
_____
_____
_____
_____

today, i must do...

_____
_____
_____
_____
_____

notes

_____
_____
_____
_____
_____
_____
_____
_____
_____
_____
_____

6AM _____

7AM _____

8AM _____

9AM _____

10AM _____

11AM _____

12PM _____

1PM _____

2PM _____

3PM _____

4PM _____

5PM _____

6PM _____

7PM _____

8PM _____

My Prayer Journal date :_____

Confession

_____
_____
_____
_____
_____
_____
_____
_____
_____

Things I'm Thankful for

_____
_____
_____
_____
_____
_____
_____
_____
_____

Prayers for Others

_____
_____
_____
_____
_____
_____
_____
_____
_____
_____

Prayers for Myself

_____
_____
_____
_____
_____
_____
_____
_____
_____
_____

Date: _____

INSIGHTS FOR THE DAY:

_____

_____

_____

_____

_____

NOTES:

_____

_____

_____

_____

_____

_____

_____

_____

_____

_____

_____

_____

_____

_____

_____

_____

_____

My Daily Schedule

today, i must contact...

today, i must do...

notes

6AM

7AM

8AM

9AM

10AM

11AM

12PM

1PM

2PM

3PM

4PM

5PM

6PM

7PM

8PM

My Prayer Journal date :_____

Confession

_____

Things I'm Thankful for

_____

Prayers for Others

_____

Prayers for Myself

_____

Date: _____

INSIGHTS FOR THE DAY:

_____

_____

_____

_____

_____

NOTES:

_____

_____

_____

_____

_____

_____

_____

_____

_____

_____

_____

_____

_____

_____

_____

_____

My Daily Schedule

today, i must contact...

_____
_____
_____
_____
_____
_____

today, i must do...

_____
_____
_____
_____
_____
_____

notes

_____
_____
_____
_____
_____
_____
_____
_____
_____
_____
_____
_____

6AM
7AM
8AM
9AM
10AM
11AM
12PM
1PM
2PM
3PM
4PM
5PM
6PM
7PM
8PM

My Prayer Journal date :_____

Confession

_____
_____
_____
_____
_____
_____
_____
_____

Things I'm Thankful for

_____
_____
_____
_____
_____
_____
_____
_____

Prayers for Others

_____
_____
_____
_____
_____
_____
_____
_____
_____

Prayers for Myself

_____
_____
_____
_____
_____
_____
_____
_____
_____

Date: _____

INSIGHTS FOR THE DAY:

_____

_____

_____

_____

_____

NOTES:

_____

_____

_____

_____

_____

_____

_____

_____

_____

_____

_____

_____

_____

_____

_____

My Daily Schedule

today, i must contact...

today, i must do...

notes

6AM

7AM

8AM

9AM

10AM

11AM

12PM

1PM

2PM

3PM

4PM

5PM

6PM

7PM

8PM

My Prayer Journal date :_____

Confession

_____
_____
_____
_____
_____
_____
_____
_____
_____

Things I'm Thankful for

_____
_____
_____
_____
_____
_____
_____
_____
_____

Prayers for Others

_____
_____
_____
_____
_____
_____
_____

Prayers for Myself

_____
_____
_____
_____
_____
_____
_____

Date: _____

INSIGHTS FOR THE DAY:

_____

_____

_____

_____

_____

NOTES:

_____

_____

_____

_____

_____

_____

_____

_____

_____

_____

_____

_____

_____

_____

_____

_____

_____

My Daily Schedule

today, i must contact...

-
-
-
-
-
-

today, i must do...

-
-
-
-
-
-

notes

6AM

7AM

8AM

9AM

10AM

11AM

12PM

1PM

2PM

3PM

4PM

5PM

6PM

7PM

8PM

My Prayer Journal date :_____

Confession

Things I'm Thankful for

Prayers for Others

Prayers for Myself

Date: _____

INSIGHTS FOR THE DAY:

_____

_____

_____

_____

_____

NOTES:

_____

_____

_____

_____

_____

_____

_____

_____

_____

_____

_____

_____

_____

_____

_____

_____

_____

My Daily Schedule

today, i must contact...

today, i must do...

notes

6AM

7AM

8AM

9AM

10AM

11AM

12PM

1PM

2PM

3PM

4PM

5PM

6PM

7PM

8PM

My Prayer Journal date :_____

Confession

Things I'm Thankful for

Prayers for Others

Prayers for Myself

Date: _____

INSIGHTS FOR THE DAY:

_____

_____

_____

_____

_____

NOTES:

_____

_____

_____

_____

_____

_____

_____

_____

_____

_____

_____

_____

_____

_____

My Daily Schedule

today, i must contact...

_____
_____
_____
_____
_____

today, i must do...

_____
_____
_____
_____
_____

notes

_____
_____
_____
_____
_____
_____
_____
_____
_____

6AM
7AM
8AM
9AM
10AM
11AM
12PM
1PM
2PM
3PM
4PM
5PM
6PM
7PM
8PM

My Prayer Journal date : _____

Confession

Things I'm Thankful for

Prayers for Others

Prayers for Myself

Date: _____

INSIGHTS FOR THE DAY:

_____

_____

_____

_____

_____

NOTES:

_____

_____

_____

_____

_____

_____

_____

_____

_____

_____

_____

_____

_____

_____

_____

_____

_____

My Daily Schedule

today, i must contact...

today, i must do...

notes

6AM

7AM

8AM

9AM

10AM

11AM

12PM

1PM

2PM

3PM

4PM

5PM

6PM

7PM

8PM

My Prayer Journal date :_____

Confession

_____
_____
_____
_____
_____
_____
_____
_____
_____

Things I'm Thankful for

_____
_____
_____
_____
_____
_____
_____
_____
_____

Prayers for Others

_____
_____
_____
_____
_____
_____
_____

Prayers for Myself

_____
_____
_____
_____
_____
_____
_____

Date: _____

INSIGHTS FOR THE DAY:

_____

_____

_____

_____

_____

NOTES:

_____

_____

_____

_____

_____

_____

_____

_____

_____

_____

_____

_____

_____

_____

_____

_____

My Daily Schedule

today, i must contact...

-
-
-
-
-
-

today, i must do...

-
-
-
-
-
-

notes

6AM

7AM

8AM

9AM

10AM

11AM

12PM

1PM

2PM

3PM

4PM

5PM

6PM

7PM

8PM

My Prayer Journal date :_____

Confession

_____
_____
_____
_____
_____
_____
_____
_____

Things I'm Thankful for

_____
_____
_____
_____
_____
_____
_____
_____
_____

Prayers for Others

_____
_____
_____
_____
_____
_____
_____
_____

Prayers for Myself

_____
_____
_____
_____
_____
_____
_____
_____

Date: _____

INSIGHTS FOR THE DAY:

_____

_____

_____

_____

_____

NOTES:

_____

_____

_____

_____

_____

_____

_____

_____

_____

_____

_____

_____

_____

My Daily Schedule

today, i must contact...

-
-
-
-
-
-

today, i must do...

-
-
-
-
-
-

notes

Time	
6AM	
7AM	
8AM	
9AM	
10AM	
11AM	
12PM	
1PM	
2PM	
3PM	
4PM	
5PM	
6PM	
7PM	
8PM	

My Prayer Journal date :_____

Confession

_____

_____

_____

_____

_____

_____

_____

_____

_____

Things I'm Thankful for

_____

_____

_____

_____

_____

_____

_____

_____

_____

_____

Prayers for Others

_____

_____

_____

_____

_____

_____

_____

_____

_____

Prayers for Myself

_____

_____

_____

_____

_____

_____

_____

_____

_____

Date: _____

INSIGHTS FOR THE DAY:

_____

_____

_____

_____

_____

NOTES:

_____

_____

_____

_____

_____

_____

_____

_____

_____

_____

_____

_____

_____

_____

_____

_____

_____

My Daily Schedule

today, i must contact...

today, i must do...

notes

6AM

7AM

8AM

9AM

10AM

11AM

12PM

1PM

2PM

3PM

4PM

5PM

6PM

7PM

8PM

My Prayer Journal date :_____

Confession

_____
_____
_____
_____
_____
_____
_____
_____

Things I'm Thankful for

_____
_____
_____
_____
_____
_____
_____
_____
_____

Prayers for Others

_____
_____
_____
_____
_____
_____

Prayers for Myself

_____
_____
_____
_____
_____
_____
_____

Date: _____

INSIGHTS FOR THE DAY:

_____

_____

_____

_____

_____

NOTES:

_____

_____

_____

_____

_____

_____

_____

_____

_____

_____

_____

_____

_____

_____

_____

_____

_____

My Daily Schedule

today, i must contact...

-
-
-
-
-

today, i must do...

-
-
-
-
-
-

notes

6AM

7AM

8AM

9AM

10AM

11AM

12PM

1PM

2PM

3PM

4PM

5PM

6PM

7PM

8PM

My Prayer Journal date :_____

Confession

_____

_____

_____

_____

_____

_____

_____

_____

Things I'm Thankful for

_____

_____

_____

_____

_____

_____

_____

_____

_____

Prayers for Others

_____

_____

_____

_____

_____

_____

_____

Prayers for Myself

_____

_____

_____

_____

_____

_____

_____

Date: _____

INSIGHTS FOR THE DAY:

_____

_____

_____

_____

_____

NOTES:

_____

_____

_____

_____

_____

_____

_____

_____

_____

_____

_____

_____

_____

_____

_____

_____

_____

My Daily Schedule

today, i must contact...

_____
_____
_____
_____
_____
_____

today, i must do...

_____
_____
_____
_____
_____
_____

notes

_____
_____
_____
_____
_____
_____
_____
_____
_____
_____

6AM
7AM
8AM
9AM
10AM
11AM
12PM
1PM
2PM
3PM
4PM
5PM
6PM
7PM
8PM

My Prayer Journal date :_____

Confession

Things I'm Thankful for

Prayers for Others

Prayers for Myself

Date: _____

INSIGHTS FOR THE DAY:

_____

_____

_____

_____

_____

NOTES:

_____

_____

_____

_____

_____

_____

_____

_____

_____

_____

_____

_____

_____

My Daily Schedule

today, i must contact...

-
-
-
-
-

today, i must do...

-
-
-
-
-
-

notes

6AM

7AM

8AM

9AM

10AM

11AM

12PM

1PM

2PM

3PM

4PM

5PM

6PM

7PM

8PM

My Prayer Journal date :_____

Confession

Things I'm Thankful for

Prayers for Others

Prayers for Myself

Date: _____

INSIGHTS FOR THE DAY:

_____

_____

_____

_____

_____

NOTES:

_____

_____

_____

_____

_____

_____

_____

_____

_____

_____

_____

_____

_____

_____

_____

_____

_____

My Daily Schedule

today, i must contact...

- _____
- _____
- _____
- _____
- _____
- _____

today, i must do...

- _____
- _____
- _____
- _____
- _____
- _____

notes

_____
_____
_____
_____
_____
_____
_____
_____
_____
_____
_____

6AM _____

7AM _____

8AM _____

9AM _____

10AM _____

11AM _____

12PM _____

1PM _____

2PM _____

3PM _____

4PM _____

5PM _____

6PM _____

7PM _____

8PM _____

My Prayer Journal date :_____

Confession

_____
_____
_____
_____
_____
_____
_____
_____

Things I'm Thankful for

_____
_____
_____
_____
_____
_____
_____
_____

Prayers for Others

_____
_____
_____
_____
_____
_____
_____
_____

Prayers for Myself

_____
_____
_____
_____
_____
_____
_____
_____

Date: _____

INSIGHTS FOR THE DAY:

_____

_____

_____

_____

_____

NOTES:

_____

_____

_____

_____

_____

_____

_____

_____

_____

_____

_____

_____

_____

_____

_____

My Daily Schedule

today, i must contact...

today, i must do...

notes

6AM

7AM

8AM

9AM

10AM

11AM

12PM

1PM

2PM

3PM

4PM

5PM

6PM

7PM

8PM

My Prayer Journal date :_____

Confession

Things I'm Thankful for

Prayers for Others

Prayers for Myself

Date: _____

INSIGHTS FOR THE DAY:

_____

_____

_____

_____

_____

NOTES:

_____

_____

_____

_____

_____

_____

_____

_____

_____

_____

_____

_____

_____

_____

_____

_____

My Daily Schedule

today, i must contact...

-
-
-
-
-
-

today, i must do...

-
-
-
-
-
-

notes

6AM

7AM

8AM

9AM

10AM

11AM

12PM

1PM

2PM

3PM

4PM

5PM

6PM

7PM

8PM

My Prayer Journal date :_____

Confession

_____
_____
_____
_____
_____
_____
_____
_____
_____

Things I'm Thankful for

_____
_____
_____
_____
_____
_____
_____
_____
_____
_____

Prayers for Others

_____
_____
_____
_____
_____
_____
_____

Prayers for Myself

_____
_____
_____
_____
_____
_____
_____

Date: _____

INSIGHTS FOR THE DAY:

_____

_____

_____

_____

_____

NOTES:

_____

_____

_____

_____

_____

_____

_____

_____

_____

_____

_____

_____

_____

_____

_____

_____

My Daily Schedule

today, i must contact...

-
-
-
-
-

today, i must do...

-
-
-
-
-
-

notes

6AM

7AM

8AM

9AM

10AM

11AM

12PM

1PM

2PM

3PM

4PM

5PM

6PM

7PM

8PM

My Prayer Journal date :_____

Confession

Things I'm Thankful for

Prayers for Others

Prayers for Myself

Date: _____

INSIGHTS FOR THE DAY:

_____

_____

_____

_____

_____

NOTES:

_____

_____

_____

_____

_____

_____

_____

_____

_____

_____

_____

_____

_____

_____

_____

_____

My Daily Schedule

today, i must contact...

today, i must do...

notes

- 6AM
- 7AM
- 8AM
- 9AM
- 10AM
- 11AM
- 12PM
- 1PM
- 2PM
- 3PM
- 4PM
- 5PM
- 6PM
- 7PM
- 8PM

My Prayer Journal date :_____

Confession

Things I'm Thankful for

Prayers for Others

Prayers for Myself

Date: _____

INSIGHTS FOR THE DAY:

_____

_____

_____

_____

_____

NOTES:

_____

_____

_____

_____

_____

_____

_____

_____

_____

_____

_____

_____

_____

_____

_____

_____

My Daily Schedule

today, i must contact...

-
-
-
-
-
-

today, i must do...

-
-
-
-
-
-

notes

6AM

7AM

8AM

9AM

10AM

11AM

12PM

1PM

2PM

3PM

4PM

5PM

6PM

7PM

8PM

My Prayer Journal date :_____

Confession

Things I'm Thankful for

Prayers for Others

Prayers for Myself

Date: _____

INSIGHTS FOR THE DAY:

_____

_____

_____

_____

_____

NOTES:

_____

_____

_____

_____

_____

_____

_____

_____

_____

_____

_____

_____

_____

_____

_____

_____

My Daily Schedule

today, i must contact...

today, i must do...

notes

6AM

7AM

8AM

9AM

10AM

11AM

12PM

1PM

2PM

3PM

4PM

5PM

6PM

7PM

8PM

My Prayer Journal date :_____

Confession

_____
_____
_____
_____
_____
_____
_____
_____
_____

Things I'm Thankful for

_____
_____
_____
_____
_____
_____
_____
_____
_____
_____

Prayers for Others

_____
_____
_____
_____
_____
_____
_____
_____
_____

Prayers for Myself

_____
_____
_____
_____
_____
_____
_____
_____
_____

Date: _____

INSIGHTS FOR THE DAY:

_____

_____

_____

_____

_____

NOTES:

_____

_____

_____

_____

_____

_____

_____

_____

_____

_____

_____

_____

_____

_____

_____

My Daily Schedule

today, i must contact...

today, i must do...

notes

6AM

7AM

8AM

9AM

10AM

11AM

12PM

1PM

2PM

3PM

4PM

5PM

6PM

7PM

8PM

My Prayer Journal date :_____

Confession

Things I'm Thankful for

Prayers for Others

Prayers for Myself

Date: _____

INSIGHTS FOR THE DAY:

_____

_____

_____

_____

_____

NOTES:

_____

_____

_____

_____

_____

_____

_____

_____

_____

_____

_____

_____

_____

_____

_____

_____

My Daily Schedule

today, i must contact...

- _____
- _____
- _____
- _____
- _____
- _____

today, i must do...

- _____
- _____
- _____
- _____
- _____
- _____

notes

_____
_____
_____
_____
_____
_____
_____
_____
_____
_____
_____
_____

6AM _____
7AM _____
8AM _____
9AM _____
10AM _____
11AM _____
12PM _____
1PM _____
2PM _____
3PM _____
4PM _____
5PM _____
6PM _____
7PM _____
8PM _____

My Prayer Journal date :_____

Confession

Things I'm Thankful for

Prayers for Others

Prayers for Myself

Date: _____

INSIGHTS FOR THE DAY:

_____

_____

_____

_____

_____

NOTES:

_____

_____

_____

_____

_____

_____

_____

_____

_____

_____

_____

_____

_____

_____

_____

My Daily Schedule

today, i must contact...

-
-
-
-
-
-

today, i must do...

-
-
-
-
-
-

notes

6AM

7AM

8AM

9AM

10AM

11AM

12PM

1PM

2PM

3PM

4PM

5PM

6PM

7PM

8PM

My Prayer Journal date :_____

Confession

Things I'm Thankful for

Prayers for Others

Prayers for Myself

Date: _____

INSIGHTS FOR THE DAY:

_____

_____

_____

_____

_____

NOTES:

_____

_____

_____

_____

_____

_____

_____

_____

_____

_____

_____

_____

_____

_____

_____

My Daily Schedule

today, i must contact...

-
-
-
-
-
-

today, i must do...

-
-
-
-
-
-

notes

6AM

7AM

8AM

9AM

10AM

11AM

12PM

1PM

2PM

3PM

4PM

5PM

6PM

7PM

8PM

My Prayer Journal date :_____

Confession
_____
_____
_____
_____
_____
_____
_____
_____
_____

Things I'm Thankful for
_____
_____
_____
_____
_____
_____
_____
_____
_____

Prayers for Others
_____
_____
_____
_____
_____
_____
_____
_____
_____

Prayers for Myself
_____
_____
_____
_____
_____
_____
_____
_____
_____

Date: _____

INSIGHTS FOR THE DAY:

_____

_____

_____

_____

_____

NOTES:

_____

_____

_____

_____

_____

_____

_____

_____

_____

_____

_____

_____

_____

_____

_____

My Daily Schedule

today, i must contact...

-
-
-
-
-
-

today, i must do...

-
-
-
-
-
-

notes

6AM

7AM

8AM

9AM

10AM

11AM

12PM

1PM

2PM

3PM

4PM

5PM

6PM

7PM

8PM

www.ingramcontent.com/pod-product-compliance
Lightning Source LLC
Chambersburg PA
CBHW080738250626
47170CB00010B/2878